What you can watch on Amazon Fire Stick?

Amazon Fire Stick is a small device which looks like flash drive which can be plugged into a TV HDMI port. This device is manufactured by Amazon and was released on April 2, 2014, With the help of this device you can stream TV contents over Wi-Fi. Such as YouTube, Netflix, Hulu, Pandopra, HBO GO and much more.

There is a remote control which comes with this device which has buttons and a button to Alexa Voice Assistant.

To use Amazon fire stick you need the following:

- Amazon account
- Wireless Internet Connection
- HD TV
- Fire Stick device with equipments:
  Fire TV stick Device

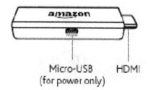

Micro-USB   HDMI
(for power only)

Amazon Fire TV remote

Navigation
Select
Menu
Home
Back
Rewind
Play/Pause
Fast Forward

amazon

Power Adapter

USB Power Cable

USB cable
(for power)

HDMI Extender Cable

HDMI
extender
cable

The above-mentioned equipment comes with the Amazon fire TV package except for High Definition TV.

Setting up Fire TV Stick

1. First, plug in the smaller end of the USB power into the Fire stick device and another end into the power adapter. After that plug the adapter into the power source.
2. Now plug the fire stick into the HDMI port of your TV. You can also use the HDMI extender to plug the port into the TV after connecting it to the fire stick port.
3. Turn on the TV and select the HDMI input source
4. Now insert 2 AAA batteries into the Amazon fire stick TV remote.
5. Once the batteries are inserted, the Amazon fire TV remote automatically becomes 'discoverable" and it will automatically get paired with the Fire Stick TV.

Setting up a Wireless connection:

1. From the home screen, select Settings>System>wifi. Your fire stick device will automatically detect the wifi network, simply select your Wi-Fi network and enter your wifi password to connect.
2. Once connected press Home button and it will display the Home screen.

Connecting to a public wifi network

If you are traveling or staying in hotels there also you can connect your amazon fire TV stick. But in this case, you will require browser login.

1 In the Home screen, select Select Settings>System>wifi.
2 In the Available Networks select public Wi-Fi network.
3. Follow the on-screen instructions to connect to the wi-fi.
4. Once the device is connected to the network, the browser window will close automatically.

Watch Movies & TV Shows:

With Amazon fire stick you can buy or rent and stream Amazon instant video movies and TV shows. You can also watch movies and TV shows through third-party apps like Hulu or Netflix.

Buy or Rent Movies &TV shows

You can watch purchased or rented movies or TV shows. Once purchased or rented it can be accessed from Your Video Library. And you can watch them as often as you like. The movies and TV shows from third-party apps, like Netflix and Hulu, can be watched directly from the apps.

1. Simply browse through the categories under Movies and TV.

2. Search for a movie or TV show there are three ways to search:

- Through Amazon Fire TV remote: simply press the voice button on your remote and then say your title name or character name or genre. Or simply select search button from the home screen.

- Through Fire TV Remote App: to do this press the Voice icon, drag the icon down, and after that say the titles name, character name, or genre. You will also be able to use the keyboard icon to use an onscreen keyboard.

- Though Amazon Fire TV Remote: select search from the home screen and use the onscreen keyboard.

3. Once the search is performed simply select the movie or TV show to view its detail such as release date and price to rent or to buy.

4. Now select Buy or Rent and follow the on-screen instructions. Once purchased it will appear on Your Video Library section if it is purchased from Amazon Instant video. If it is available in another service's catalog then

the app will automatically open up so that you can watch the content.

5. Once purchased select Watch Now button to immediately watch the movie or TV show from your Amazon Fire TV device.

Watch Movies & TV Shows

With the help of Amazon Fire TV, you can buy, rent and stream Amazon instant video movies and TV shows. You can also watch movies and TV shows with the help of third-party apps like Netflix or Hulu.

Buy or Rent Movies & TV Shows

When you rent videos from Amazon Instant video, you will be able to watch them for a specified time period. When you purchase videos from Amazon Instant Videos you can access them from Your Video Library.

To do this simply follow these steps:

1. Simply browse through the categories under Movies or TV. now search for a movie or TV

shows you can search for movies or TV shows by the following two methods:

a. Using Amazon Fire TV Voice Remote:

Simply press and hold Voice 🎤 button on your remote, once pressed say a title, actor name, character name, or genre. Or simply select Search from the Home Screen.

b. Using Fire TV Remote App: to do this

simply press and hold Voice 🎤 icon, drag the icon down, and then say a title, actor name, character name, or genre.

c. Using Amazon Fire TV remote: Simply select Search from the Home screen once selected you can use the onscreen keyboard to enter search items.

2. Once the search is done you can select the movies or TV show to view its detailed description.

3. Once your desired movies or TV shows is selected you will select Buy or Rent and simply follow the on-screen instructions. If you have purchased your video from Amazon Instant Videos, your purchase will appear in Your Video Library. If the video is purchased from another service's catalog the app will automatically open so you can watch it from there.

4. Finally, select Watch Now to watch the movie or TV show from your amazon fire TV device.

How to Watch Movies and TV Shows:

You can watch TV or Movies by two options as detailed below:

If you have purchased or rented a video in Amazon instant Video you will be able to watch it by going to Video Library, if you have purchased or rented your video through 3rd party apps then you will have to open the 3rd party app to access the video or TV show or movie.

- To watch Amazon Instant Video movies or TV shows:

   a. Simply select Video Library form the Home screen,
   b. Now, select the movie or TV show you want to watch and select Watch Now or Resume to begin streaming the movie or TV show.

- To watch Prime Instant Video movies or TV shows:
   a. In the home screen simply go to Prime Video category. Here you can browse the Recently Added to Prime or Top Movies

and TV on Prime lists on home screen or in the Movies and TV categories.

b. Simply select the movies or TV show you want to watch and select the video art work to start streaming the b movie or TV show at no additional costs. (In order to watch the movies or TV shows for free you need to be an Amazon Prime member.)

How to use an Amazon Fire TV Device with a Second Screen Device?

With the help of this feature, you can easily share your screen to second screen device. In this way, you will be able to pass videos and photos from your compatible device.

The second screen is compatible with these devices:

- Kindle Fire HD 2nd generation
- Kindle Fire HDX
- Fire HD 6
- Fire HD 7
- Amazon Fire phone

Before you start using this feature you need to connect both your devices to the internet. Make sure that both your devices are connected to the same network. Also, make sure that both the devices are connected to the same Amazon account.

Also, make sure that you have turned on the screen notifications.

To do this simply go to Settings> Display and Sounds> Second Screen Notifications.

- For Amazon Instant Video movies or TV shows:
  a. On your tablet first, find an Amazon Instant Video or TV you want to watch.

b. Now tap on Send To ⬆ icon and after that select your Amazon Fire TV device from the list. Once done the video will start playing on your TV

c. Once the video starts playing you can control playback by tapping the Play ▶, Pause ❚❚, or Jump Back ↺ buttons.

- For photos or personal videos:

a. On your tablet, simply tap Photos.

b. Now simply swipe from the left edge on the screen and after that select a category under Library or select a specific photo album. there you will see the Send To ⬆ icon in the top right.

c. Finally, tap the Send To ⬆ icon to display the album on your TV.

How to use Amazon Fire TV Device as a display Mirroring Destination?

Using this feature you can wirelessly display your compatible phone or tablet screen and audio on your Amazon Fire TV device.

Following are the compatible devices to which you can mirror your display:

- Fire phone
- Fire HDX Tablets
- Devices running Android 4.2 (Jelly Bean) or higher

Before mirroring your device make sure your Amazon Fire TV device Miracast capable device are turned on and are within 30 feet of each other. Also, make sure both the devices are connected to the same Amazon account and the wi-fi network is the same.

Fire HDX Tablet:

1. First swipe down from the top of the screen to open Quick Settings, after that tap Settings.
2. Now Tap Display & Sounds and after that tap Display Mirroring.

3. Now select your Amazon Firer TV device. It will take 20 seconds for your Fire tablet screen to appear on your TV screen. Once done the mirroring will start, to stop mirroring your Fire tablet tap Stop Mirroring.

Fire phone

1. First, open quick Actions.
2. Now under Display select Share your screen via Miracast.
3. Now select your Amazon Fire TV device. After that, it will take 20 seconds for your fire phone screen to appear on your TV screen.
4. Once done mirroring will start. To Stop Mirroring, tap on Stop Mirroring.

Android device running 4.2 or higher:

1. On your Amazon fire TV device, simply select Settings>Display and Sounds> Enable Display Mirroring.
2. Once done, on your Miracast- certified device, connect to your Amazon Fire TV.
3. Now press any button on the remote to stop display Mirroring.

How to turn On or Customize Closed Captions?

To watch a video with closed captions:

1. Select and play the video you want to watch.
2. Once video playback has started, press the menu ⌖ button on the remote or in the fire TV remote app and then select **Turn captions on.**
3. Then press the menu ⌖ button again to get back to video playback with captions on.
4. To turn captions off, Press the **Menu** ⌖ button again on the remote, and then select **Turn captions off.**

How to view scene and actor information on Amazon Fire TV Devices?

X-ray helps you discover and learn more about actors and characters in a scene while watching movies and TV shows on your Amazon Fire TV device. X-ray also identifies music in the scene as it plays. X-ray is available on Amazon Fire TV and Fire TV stick.

How to view X-ray information on your Amazon fire TV device when an x-ray supported video is playing:

- To peek at information about the current scene, such as the involved actors or song playing, and continue video playback:
    1. Open X-ray Quick view, then press up or pause on your amazon remote.

    Tip- press down to hide X-ray quick view.

- To look at in-depth information about songs and actors, as well as trivia – Open full-screen x-ray:
    1. Open x-ray quick view by pressing pause or up on your Amazon remote.
    2. Then press up.

- To skip between scenes:
    1. Open x-ray quick view by pressing up or pause on your Amazon remote.
    2. Then press up to open full-screen x-ray.
    3. Then to select scenes, scroll through the video tiles.

- To resume video and close full screen x-ray:

    Press play on your Amazon remote.

Play games and apps.

How to buy, download and uninstall games and apps?

- Search and locate the game or app with an app or remote or browse the categories under Games or Apps.

  a) **Amazon fire TV remote:** select search from the home screen and use the onscreen keyboard to enter search terms.

  b) **Amazon fire TV voice remote:** press the voice 🎤 button on your remote to search using your voice or press up or select search from the home screen to use an onscreen keyboard.

  c) **Fire TV remote app:** press and hold the voice 🎤 icon, then drag the icon down, to say the name of an app or game. Or you can also tap the keyboard icon to use an onscreen keyboard.

- Now from your search results, select a game or app to view its overview page. Now you can see the works with a box on the overview page. Here you can also see the system and controller compatibility:

    a) **All**
    b) **Fire TV Stick** (visible on fire TV stick)
    c) **Fire TV remote** (Amazon fire TV remote and Amazon fire TV voice remote)
    d) **Amazon fire game controller**
    e) **Tablet games on fire TV** (requires a mouse or a game controller)

- Now select buy or free if the app is free. Once purchased, your game or app begins downloading automatically. When the download is complete, the button will change to open.

- Now select open to start using your game or app.

  Tip- The games or apps you purchase are available in your games library or apps library.

  ### How to uninstall apps and games?

  You can uninstall games and apps from your Amazon fire TV device or USB storage also the games and apps you purchased can be reinstalled again from the overview page if you uninstalled it.
- Select **settings > manage all applications,** from your home screen.

Select **USB storage** or **fire TV** to see apps that are only stored in USB storage.

- To find the app you want to uninstall, scroll up or down and select it.
- Then select **uninstall,** and follow the onscreen instructions.

How to play games and apps?

Your purchased and downloaded games and apps can be found in your games library or your apps library.

Filter the search results by:

a) **All**

b) **Fire TV Stick** (visible on fire TV stick)

c) **Fire TV remote** (Amazon fire TV remote and Amazon fire TV voice remote)

d) **Amazon fire game controller**

e) **Tablet games on fire TV** (requires a mouse or a game controller)

How to find which controllers are compatible with the game?

a) Navigate to a game and select **more info.**
b) You will see controller information in the **works with** box.

Launch a game or app.

a) Go to home screen and select **games or apps.**
b) Now you'll find your purchased games and apps in your games library or your apps library.
c) Select the game or app to start using or playing the game or app.

How to play tablet games on amazon fire TV devices?

These games require an Amazon fire game controller or mouse to be played.

How to find a tablet style game?

a) Select games, from the home screen.

b) Filter by tablet games on fire TV.

To play tablet style game with a game controller:

- Left joystick: move "mouse" pointer
- **A** button: a single click or tap
- **B** button: back
- Right shoulder button: increase cursor speed
- Left shoulder button: decrease cursor speed

To play a tablet style game with a mouse:

- Left click: a single tap or click.
- Mouse movement: move "mouse" pointer.

<u>How to turn off In-App purchasing?</u>

- Go to home screen and select **settings > parental controls.**
- Then press the **select** button again to change the button to **on.**
- Now enter your amazon parental controls pin (if you already have one) or create a new one, and then select **next.**
- Now select PIN protect purchases to change the button to ON.
- With parental controls enabled, all purchases will require a PIN.

Note: If you forget your PIN, visit http://www.amazon.com/PIN to reset your Parental Controls PIN.

What is gamecircle?

Amazon Gamecircle enhances your gaming experience by storing high scores, achievements and time played in the cloud, so you can compare with other gamecircle users and friends.

Press the Home ⌂ button on your remote or press the

Gamecircle ⊙ button on your Amazon fire game controller to see more information about gamecircle – enabled game.

How to hide your Gamecircle profile?

Now you can hide your gaming information from the Gamecircle settings screen.

- Go to home screen, then select settings > applications > Amazon Gamecircle.
- Select share your gamecircle Nickname so that the feature will turn off.

How to listen to music?

Now you can listen to songs purchased from the digital music store or imported to your music library on your Amazon fire TV device with Amazon Music. You can also view lyrics with x-ray for music if available.

Listen to music

a) Go to home screen and select music.
b) Now browse for music you want to play in the recently played list or browse by playlists, artists, albums or genres.
c) Select the song, or playlist to start playing. Use the playback controls on the remote or in the Fire TV remote app to play, pause, forward or rewind the music.

Tip: you can exit to the home screen at any time and the music will keep playing while you view photos or play games. Also, you can continue to use the playback controls on the remote.

How to view song Lyrics?

1. How to find songs with lyrics?
   a) Go to Home screen and select Music.
   b) Browse your album or search for an album. Or press and hold the voice ⊕ button and then say the album title.
   c) In the list of songs in the album, songs that have

lyrics appear with
[+lyrics].

2. Press down or up on the
   remote to scroll ahead and
   back through the lyrics, while a
   song is playing and the lyrics
   are displayed. You can also
   press select to jump to that
   section of the song.

How to listen to prime music with an Amazon Fire TV device?

Now you can listen to Prime music from
your Amazon Fire TV device.

To listen you must be an active Prime member.

How to listen to prime music?

1. Go to home screen and select Music.
2. Go to your prime playlists or browse to a prime album in your albums.
3. Select the song, or playlist to start playing. Use the playback controls on the remote or in the Fire TV remote app to play, pause, forward or rewind the music.

Manage Photos and Screensavers

Your cloud drive photos and personal videos are available on your Amazon fire TV device when you register your Amazon Fire TV device to your Amazon account.

View Photos and Personal Videos

1. How to view photos and personal videos from your cloud drive:
   a) Go to home screen and select photos.
   b) Navigate the lists:
      - **All** – scroll left and right to view thumbnails of all of yours photos and videos. Select a photo or video to view the full sized version then scroll left and right to continue viewing

the full sized
versions of your
photos and videos.
Press the back ⊖
button to return to
the thumbnails.

- **Favorites** – To add
  an item, select add
  to favorites below
  any photo or video.
- **Albums**- select
  album to view
  photos and videos
  in it.
- **Videos**- select a
  video to play it and
  use the playback
  controls on the
  remote to pause,
  play, rewind and
  forward.

1. How to view photos and personal videos directly from your compatible device:

    a) Compatible fire devices

    - FIRE HD 6
    - FIRE HD 7
    - KINDLE FIRE HD 2nd GENERATION
    - KINDLE FIRE HDX
    - AMAZON FIRE PHONE
        b) Swipe from left edge of the screen, and select category or album.
        c) Then tap the second screen icon at the top to display your photos or videos on your TV.

View slideshows

You can view full-screen slideshow of your photos on your Amazon fire TV device.

1. Go to home screen and select photos.
2. Then select any album and select start slideshow.
   - The slideshow automatically advances through photos and videos located in the list you are viewing.

- Your slideshow automatically restarts when it reaches the end.
- You can also press left or right to go forward or back in the album at your own speed.

How to add Photos and Personal Videos to Cloud Drive?

1. Go to home screen, select Photos>add photos and videos.
2. Follow the instructions on the screen:
   a) Select Get the mobile app for iOS or Android.
   b) Then enter your mobile number to receive a text message with a link to install the app.
   c) When you receive the message open it and tap the link to automatically go to the cloud drive app in the app store or google play store.
   Select send again or send to a different number if you don't receive the message.
   d) After installing the app, open it and sign in with your Amazon account.

e) Accept and turn on auto save. This will allow the photos and videos on your mobile device to be added to your Amazon cloud drive and will be available on your Amazon Fire TV device.

Tip - You can also download the mobile app from www.amazon.com/clouddriveapp

How to set screen savers?

1. Go to Home screen, select photos to view your photo albums.
2. Then select a photo or album and then select set as screen saver.
3. You can also change your screen saver settings, such as the slide style, slide speed, and start time.
   The screen saver will launch when you left your Fire device idle.

How to manage subscriptions of your Amazon Fire TV device?

There are some subscriptions that you can sign up on your Amazon Fire TV device without visit any third party website.

You must create a new username and password for the subscription while you are signing up.

How to manage one of these subscriptions:

1. Go to
   www.amazon.com/appstoresubscriptions
   and use your username and password to sign in.
2. Select Actions and then management option, next to the subscription.
   - **Edit payment information**
   - **View billing history**
   - **Cancel your subscription**

How to share Content on Amazon Fire TV Devices?

Use family library on your Amazon Fire TV device to share your apps and games with others in an Amazon household.

- Go to **settings > account > sync content**

  The following content can be shared in a household on Amazon Fire TV devices:

a) Free and purchased apps compatible with Amazon Fire TV devices.
b) Free and purchased games compatible with Amazon Fire TV devices.

The following content cannot be shared in a household on Amazon Fire TV devices:

a) Prime instant video
b) Prime music
c) Purchased Amazon music
d) Purchased Amazon instant videos
e) Third party App content or information
f) Games and apps on USB storage.

How to use Amazon Fire TV Devices in a different country?

Your Amazon Fire TV device will work in the following countries:

- United States
- United Kingdom (UK)
- Germany
- Austria (Fire TV stick only)

In order to use your device outside of the U.S. you need to change the country settings to your Amazon account.

How to change your country settings?

1. Go to the settings tab in manage your content and devices.
2. Under country settings select change.
3. Enter your new address
4. Choose a supported country and then select update.
5. Select learn more in the notification area and then select transfer your kindle account to.
6. On your Fire TV device, go to Home > settings > my account. Select deregister. And then return to my account and select register.

Now your Amazon Fire TV is ready to use in the supported country.